Artists in Their Time

Marc Chagall

Jude Welton

Franklin Watts
A Division of Scholastic Inc.
New York Toronto London Auckland Sydney
Mexico City   New Delhi   Hong Kong
Danbury, Connecticut

To the memory of
Richard Widdows (1947-2002)
A great editor, mentor, and friend

First published in 2003 by
Franklin Watts
96 Leonard Street
London EC2A 4XD

First American edition published
in 2003 by Franklin Watts
A Division of Scholastic Inc.
90 Sherman Turnpike
Danbury, CT 06816

Series Editor: Adrian Cole
Series Designer: Mo Choy
Art Director: Jonathan Hair
Picture Researcher: Diana Morris

A CIP catalog record for this title
is available from the Library of Congress.

ISBN 0-531-12235-2 (Lib. Bdg.)
ISBN 0-531-16645-7 (Pbk.)

Printed in Hong Kong, China

Acknowledgements

AKG London: 24t, 24c, 28c, 30t. photograph © 2002 The Art Institute of Chicago. All rights reserved. Gift of Alfred S. Alschuler, 1946.925: 29 © ADAGP, Paris & DACS, London 2003. photograph © 2002 The Art Institute of Chicago. All rights reserved. Gift of Mrs Gilbert W. Chapman, 1952-1005: 31 © ADAGP, Paris & DACS, London 2003. © Branger-Viollet: front cover bc & 15b. Bridgeman Art Library: 36b © ADAGP, Paris & DACS, London 2003. Buehrle Collection, Zurich/AKG London: 8b © ADAGP, Paris & DACS, London 2003. Chicester Cathedral/Bridgeman Art Library: 39 © ADAGP, Paris & DACS, London 2003. photo CNAC/MNAM. Dist. RMN: 21 © ADAGP, Paris & DACS, London 2003, 25 © ADAGP, Paris & DACS, London 2003, front cover c & 35 © ADAGP, Paris & DACS, London 2003. photo Darius: 41. photo Claude Gaspari: 41t Marc Chagall & Yvette Cauquil Prince © ADAGP, Paris & DACS, London 2003. Hulton Archive: 16t, 28t, 32b. Lotte Jacobi/AKG London: 34. David King Collection: 18b, 22t, 22b, 23. Galerie Koller, Zurich: 38t © ADAGP, Paris & DACS, London 2003. Kunsthaus, Zurich/Artothek: 16c. Kunstsammlung Nordrhein-Westfalen, Dusseldorf/AKG London: 15t. Kunstsammlung Nordrhein-Westfalen, Dusseldorf/Bridgeman Art Library: 10t © ADAGP, Paris & DACS, London 2003. Edwin Levick/Hulton Archive: 32t. Walter Limot/AKG London: 14. © Lipnitzki-Viollet: front cover br & 26t, 34b, 36c. © Martinie-Viollet: 12t. Pierre Matisse Gallery Archives, The Pierpont Morgan Library, New York: 30b. Musée des Beaux-Arts, Grenoble/Artothek: 12b © L & M Services, Amsterdam 2003. Musée Message Biblique-Chagall, Nice/photo RMN-Gérard Blot: 37 © ADAGP, Paris & DACS, London 2003, 40 © ADAGP, Paris & DACS, London 2003. Museum of Art, Tel Aviv/Bridgeman Art Library: 27 © ADAGP, Paris & DACS, London 2003. Museum of the City of New York/Byron Collection/Hulton Archive: 33. Museum of Modern Art, New York/Scala, Florence: 11 © ADAGP, Paris & DACS, London 2003, 19 © ADAGP, Paris & DACS, London 2003, 20t. ND Roger-Viollet: 10b. Novosti, London: 8b, 18t, 38b. Private Collection/Bridgeman Art Library: 40 © ADAGP, Paris & DACS, London 2003. John Silver/Hutchison: 26b. Stedelijk Museum, Amsterdam/Artothek: 13 © ADAGP, Paris & DACS, London 2003. Stedelijk Museum, Amsterdam, on loan from Netherlands Institute for Cultural Heritage: 17 © ADAGP, Paris & DACS, London 2003. © Collection Viollet: front cover bl & 8t.

Whilst every attempt has been made to clear copyright
should there be any inadvertent omission please apply
in the first instance to the publisher regarding rectification.

Contents

Who Was Marc Chagall?

◀ The Segal family, c. 1910. Moyshe Segal (Marc Chagall) stands top left, his mother is seated below him and to the right, and his father is next to her.

Marc Chagall was one of the most popular and distinctive artists of the 20th century. His colorful, dreamlike works offer a unique mixture of fantasy, folklore, myth, and memory.

Marc Chagall is a French name adopted by the artist as a young man. He was born Moyshe Segal on July 7, 1887, into a large, poor Jewish family in Vitebsk, a town in western Russia. His Russian Jewish heritage was important to his life and art.

> *"Were I not a Jew, I would not have become an artist."*
>
> Marc Chagall

EARLY LIFE

Almost everything we know about Chagall's early life comes from his autobiography *My Life*, written in 1922, when he was 34. According to his own account, Chagall's birth was accompanied by great drama. A large fire broke out nearby and baby Moyshe was placed in a stone trough for safety.

Chagall was the oldest of nine children. His family were Hassidic Jews, who strictly observed their religious laws and traditions. Every day at dawn his father went to the synagogue before spending the day working for a herring merchant. His mother ran a grocery store that sold "herrings in barrels, sugar heaped like pointed heads, flour, candles..."

SCHOOL DAYS

Vitebsk was home to one of Russia's largest Jewish communities (see panel). Chagall attended the *heder*, which is the traditional Jewish primary school, where he learned Hebrew and Biblical history. Jewish children were banned from attending state schools but Chagall went to the local state secondary school after his mother had bribed the headmaster. Here he learned geometry and Russian. He was soon able to speak Russian as well as Yiddish which is the traditional Jewish language.

DRAWING INSPIRATION

According to Chagall, the only pictures in his home were family photographs. He claimed he had never seen a painting or drawn a picture before 1906. When he saw a fellow pupil drawing, it was a revelation and he began to draw, too. He was determined to become an artist.

The 19-year-old Chagall joined a local art school run by the Jewish artist Yehuda Pen (1854-1937). Chagall's obvious talent earned him free tuition. He took a job touching up photographs but the young artist wanted more from life. In the winter of 1906-07, with 27 rubles in his pocket, Chagall set out for St. Petersburg, the capital and cultural heart of Russia.

▲ Vitebsk, c. 1920. Memories of the town and his early life there remained very important to Chagall and his artistic imagery. He remembered its buildings as "simple and eternal."

"At Pen's I was the only one to paint in purple. That seemed so bold that from then onward I attended the school without paying."

Marc Chagall

▲ The empire of Russia lay to the east of Europe. Vitebsk – now in the independent country of Belarus – was in "the Pale of Settlement" (shown in yellow).

JEWS IN RUSSIA

At the time of Chagall's birth Russia was ruled by the Czar, or emperor. For centuries, Jews had suffered hatred, persecution, and segregation. They were only allowed to live in an area known as "the Pale of Settlement" (see map). Chagall's hometown of Vitebsk was within this area, and about 48,000 of its 65,000 inhabitants were Jews. The town was the stronghold of Hassidic Judaism, a Jewish sect founded in the 1730s by Baal-Shem Tov. His teachings are based on mystical writings known as the *Cabala*, which preach universal love. Hassidic Jews are noted for their piety and for their joyous dancing and chanting. This joy can be seen in Chagall's art along with many Jewish symbols.

Poverty in St. Petersburg

When the 20-year-old Chagall arrived in St. Petersburg, Russia, Jews were not allowed to live there without a permit. To get around this, a friend of the family had documents made stating that Chagall was working for a Vitebsk merchant. Once in the capital, Chagall posed as a servant for a wealthy lawyer in order to stay. Although he managed to keep ahead of the authorities, once he forgot to pay a necessary bribe and was thrown in prison for several weeks.

▲ A main street in St. Petersburg in the late 19th century.

LEARNING HIS TRADE

Chagall enrolled at the School of the Imperial Society for the Protection of the Fine Arts. The school's director, the painter Nicholai Roerich (1874-1947), was very encouraging. He arranged for Chagall to be exempt from military service and even organized a grant of 15 rubles per month. This was a lifeline for Chagall since he was living in desperate poverty, sharing a room and even a bed!

Chagall found the teaching at the art school boring and the atmosphere cold and depressing. After two years of copying plaster casts he had had enough – he left the school without collecting his monthly grant. After studying at a private art school for a couple of months he enrolled at the Zvantseva School run by Léon Bakst (1866-1924), now best remembered as a stage designer with the Ballets Russes, or Russian Ballet. Chagall later said that it

▲ Chagall, shortly before he moved to St. Petersburg.

TIMELINE ▶

July 7, 1887	1906	Winter 1906-07	1907	1908	1909
Moyshe Segal (Marc Chagall) born in Vitebsk.	Chagall enters Yehuda Pen's art school in Vitebsk.	Chagall moves to St. Petersburg.	Chagall enrolls at the School of the Imperial Society for the Protection of the Fine Arts.	Chagall leaves the Imperial Society school. He meets Maxim Vinaver.	Chagall enrolls at Zvantseva School. He meets Bella Rosenfeld, his future wife.

▲ Bella Rosenfeld, c. 1910-11. In his first meeting with Bella, Chagall wrote, "I have a feeling that this is my wife. Her pale complexion, her eyes. How large, round, and black they are! They are my eyes, my soul."

▶ *The Wedding* (or *Russian Wedding*), 1909. This early painting by Chagall shows a joyful scene from Vitebsk. The young artist used dark colors and painted this traditional scene from a realistic perspective. Chagall's style changed dramatically when he reached Paris.

"In France I was born for a second time."

Marc Chagall

was Bakst who made him aware of "the breath of Europe." When Bakst left for Paris, Chagall applied to go with him as his assistant. He was turned down.

BELOVED BELLA

Despite being virtually destitute, Chagall made several visits home to Vitebsk from St. Petersburg. During one of these visits, in October of 1909, he met Bella Rosenfeld (1895-1944). It was love at first sight for both of them. Bella was to become his beloved wife and muse for more than 30 years.

A FIRST PATRON

Chagall had another significant meeting in St. Petersburg. Maxim Vinaver (1863-1926) was an influential member of the Duma, or Russian parliament. Chagall described Vinaver as "almost like a father." He bought some of Chagall's paintings and sponsored the young artist. Most importantly, he allowed Chagall to travel to Paris. Vinaver paid his train fare and gave him an allowance of 40 rubles a month. In August of 1910, Moyshe Segal – by now known as Marc Chagall – arrived in Paris.

A Russian in Paris

▲ *Still Life With a Harp and a Violin,*
1912, Georges Braque.

CUBISM

Cubism was probably the most important art movement of the early 20th century. It was developed by Pablo Picasso (1881-1973) and Georges Braque (1882-1963) in Paris between 1907 and 1914. Creating a new way of representing the world around them, these artists and their followers abandoned the idea of showing objects from a single, fixed viewpoint as Western artists had done for centuries. Instead, they used multiple viewpoints so that different parts of an object could be seen at the same time. Objects in the real world were broken into fragments and put back together on the canvas.

T wenty-three years old and unable to speak French, Chagall was homesick yet very excited to be in Paris. He attended painting academies but mainly taught himself to paint by studying Old Masters in the Louvre and contemporary artists at work in the city.

NEW INFLUENCES

Two days after his arrival in Paris, Chagall visited the Salon des Indépendants and saw modern French art for the first time. He encountered the work of the Cubists (see panel) and the Fauves. The Fauves prompted Chagall to use bright and vibrant colors, while Cubism encouraged him to develop his own unique sense of perspective. In his early masterpiece *I and the Village* (opposite), Chagall blends memories of his Russian home with a fragmented sense of space that reflects his knowledge of Cubism.

"I have brought my subjects from Russia ... Paris has given them light."

Marc Chagall

▲ La Place de l'Opéra, Paris, 1910. The Opéra stands on the right.
Fifty-three years later, Chagall would paint its ceiling (see page 36).

TIMELINE ▶

1910	1911
Supported by a grant from Maxim Vinaver, Chagall moves to Paris in August. He sees modern French art for the first time and attends two private art academies.	Chagall moves into the artists' colony *La Ruche* (the Beehive, see pages 14-15). Here he meets the poets Blaise Cendrars (1887-1961) and Guillaume Apollinaire (1880-1918, see page 16).

The Fiddler, 1912-13

oil on canvas, 74 x 62 $^1/_5$ in (188 x 158 cm), Stedelijk Museum of Modern Art, Amsterdam, the Netherlands

Violinists featured prominently at births, marriages, and deaths in traditional Jewish communities, and so became an embodiment of the cycle of life. This is a fiddler on a roof, a symbol of the unstable position of Jews in society.

La Ruche – An Artists' Colony

Before they achieve financial success – if they ever do – aspiring young artists often need a cheap place to live and paint. In Paris at the beginning of the 20th century, this need was fulfilled for many by a rickety cluster of studios known as La Ruche, or the Beehive. Situated uncomfortably near the slaughterhouses in a run-down district of Paris known as the Vaurigard, La Ruche was not a sophisticated address but it was an exciting and inexpensive place to live and work.

▲ La Ruche, or the Beehive, in 1968. It is easy to see from its shape how the building got its name. The studios were saved from demolition in the 1960s. People still live and work in the studios today.

SALVAGED STUDIOS

La Ruche was the brainchild of the sculptor and painter Alfred Boucher (1850-1934), a descendant of the great 18th-century Rococo painter François Boucher (1703-70). Boucher bought a plot of land between the railroad and the slaughterhouses, and built the studios from pavilions salvaged from the Universal Exhibition that had been held in Paris in 1900. The original building was a twelve-sided, three-story "beehive" construction, with a cluster of 24 wedge-shaped studios. Eventually there were more than 140 studios on Boucher's plot.

SPACE TO LIVE AND WORK

Boucher wanted to create a community which would provide artists and writers from all over the world with the accommodation and work space they needed for a low rent – 50 to 300 francs per year, depending on size. With his grant from Maxim Vinaver of about 125 francs a month, Chagall was able to afford a large studio on the top floor with plenty of light.

Most of the inhabitants of La Ruche were foreigners – Russians, Italians, Germans, Poles, and Spaniards. It provided a welcome refuge for Jewish artists who suffered persecution and the threat of pogroms, or organized massacres of Jewish communities in Eastern Europe.

FAMOUS NEIGHBORS

An extraordinary array of artists came to La Ruche, many of whom were to become famous names in 20th-century art. Among Chagall's now celebrated neighbors were the Italian Jew Amedeo Modigliani (1884-1920) and the Lithuanian Jew Chaïm Soutine (1893-1943), the painter Fernand Léger (1881-1955), and sculptors Alexander Archipenko (1887-1964) and Jacques Lipchitz (1891-1973). Many writers, poets, and intellectuals came and went, too. Even the Russian revolutionary leader Vladimir Ilyich Lenin (1870-1924) stayed at La Ruche for a short time. It was a melting pot of radical ideas about art and politics.

▲ *Max Jacob*, 1916, Amedeo Modigliani. Modigliani created dramatic effects by elongating and simplifying the human face and body.

AN ARTIST'S IMPRESSION

Chagall's own description gives a vivid impression of the atmosphere at La Ruche: "On the floor, reproductions of El Greco and Cézanne lie cheek by jowl with the remains of a herring... In the Russian studios a slighted model can be heard sobbing, from the Italians comes the sound of guitars and singing, and from the Jews heated discussions. Meanwhile I am quite alone in my studio, working by my [gas] lamp... Two, three o'clock in the morning... Somewhere they are slaughtering cattle, the cows are lowing, and I paint them."

◀ A studio in La Ruche, 1906. The studios' shape was often compared to a wedge of brie cheese.

A Growing Reputation

▲ World War I is remembered for its trench warfare and the huge loss of life it caused.

During his time in Paris, Chagall's self-confidence grew – he was financially secure, his friends acknowledged his talent, and his work was gaining recognition. This confidence is expressed in his self-portrait shown opposite. Chagall, elegantly dressed, works at his easel in his Parisian studio with the Eiffel Tower seen through the window. His dreams of Russia are shown in a cloud to his right.

The poet and critic Guillaume Apollinaire helped establish Chagall's reputation in France and abroad. Apollinaire introduced him to the avant-garde Berlin art dealer Herwarth Walden, who was so impressed by Chagall's work that he organized a one-man show at his Berlin gallery, Der Sturm.

WORLD WAR I

In June of 1914, around the time that Chagall left Berlin for Vitebsk, Archduke Franz Ferdinand, heir to the throne of Austria-Hungary, was assassinated. Europe was already divided into two armed camps and this event triggered World War I. By August of 1914, Austria-Hungary and Germany were at war with France, Russia, and Britain. Turkey and Bulgaria later joined the German side. Japan, Italy, and the U.S. supported Britain, France, and Russia.

World War I is often called the "war to end all wars." No one had anticipated its huge cost or the vast number of casualties – over 13 million people died. The war's effect on Europe was profound. It triggered the Russian Revolution (see page 22) and left Germany defeated and in economic ruin.

◄ *Landscape With Cow and Camel*, 1914, **August Macke.** Macke (1887-1914) was part of Der Blaue Reiter (Blue Rider) group. Walden promoted the Blue Riders and other groups of avant-garde artists at his Der Sturm gallery.

RETURNING TO RUSSIA

Chagall left Paris in 1914 to attend his Berlin exhibition, which was a great success. He then traveled on to Vitebsk for what he intended to be a short vacation. World events changed his plans. While he was in Russia, World War I broke out and the Russian borders closed. Chagall was unable to leave. It was nine years before he returned to Paris.

TIMELINE ▶

May 1914	June 1914	August 1914
Chagall arranges to travel to Berlin for his first one-man exhibition at Walden's Der Sturm gallery.	Exhibition opens to good reviews. Chagall travels to Russia. Archduke Franz Ferdinand of Austria-Hungary is assassinated.	Germany invades France through Belgium. Britain declares war on Germany. World War I has begun. Chagall is stranded in Vitebsk.

Self Portrait With Seven Fingers, 1912-13

oil on canvas, 49 $\frac{3}{5}$ x 42 $\frac{1}{8}$ in (126 x 107 cm), Stedelijk Museum of Modern Art, Amsterdam, the Netherlands

Chagall shows himself painting an earlier work, *To Russia, Donkeys, and Others* (1912). Hebrew lettering on the wall above reads "Paris" and "Russia." Why seven fingers? Seven is a mystical number in Jewish symbolism and "with seven fingers" is a Yiddish expression for working "at full speed." Seven also had personal significance for Chagall since he was born on the seventh day of the seventh month of 1887.

To Russia With Love

PRE-REVOLUTIONARY RUSSIA

Before the Bolshevik Revolution of 1917, Russia was a vast empire ruled by an emperor, or Czar, who had absolute power. The Russian empire stretched from Germany to the Pacific Ocean and was made up of many national and ethnic groups. Only half of its population of 170 million was actually Russian.

While the Czar and the nobility lived in luxury, more than 80 percent of the population were peasants who, until 1861, had been "serfs." Serfs were workers who were tied to the land and the property of the landowner. Most of the families who worked on the land lived in terrible poverty. Workers in the cities had similarly miserable living conditions. Understandably, the peasants and workers were open to revolutionary ideas which gave them hope of freedom from this oppression and poverty.

◀ Chagall, his wife Bella, and their daughter Ida, 1917. Chagall had returned to Russia partly to continue his courtship of Bella. He was uncertain about the welcome he would receive from her but his devotion was amply rewarded.

Back in Vitebsk, Chagall was reunited with his beloved Bella Rosenfeld. She had also just returned home from Moscow where she had been studying acting. Bella's wealthy parents were not happy about her relationship with a poor, whimsical painter. However, Chagall and Bella were passionately in love and despite parental opposition they married in July of 1915. Their mutual love is expressed in many paintings, including *The Birthday* (opposite).

RECOGNITION AT HOME

Chagall had to do military service in the war but did not have to fight. His brother-in-law Jacob, an economist, arranged an office job in the War Economy Office in Petrograd (formerly St. Petersburg). Chagall moved there, visiting Bella as often as he could. In 1916 and 1917, he exhibited paintings in Petrograd and Moscow. By the time Chagall was 30, he was recognized as a major artist. Personal fulfillment also came when, on May 18, 1916, Bella gave birth to their daughter Ida.

▲ A group of Russian peasants walk to harvest with their scythes, c. 1900.

TIMELINE ▶

1915	April 1916	May 18, 1916	November 1916
On July 25 Chagall marries Bella Rosenfeld in Vitebsk. He moves to Petrograd to take up a position as a clerk in the press department of the War Economy Office.	Chagall shows 63 recent works in an exhibition of "Contemporary Russian Art" in Petrograd.	Chagall's daughter Ida is born.	Chagall shows 45 works at an exhibition in Moscow, as part of the avant-garde association of artists exhibiting together under the name of the "Knave of Diamonds."

The Birthday, 1915

oil on canvas, 31 $^7/_8$ x 39 $^3/_8$ in (81 x 100 cm), Museum of Modern Art, New York, New York

In this joyful, dreamlike double portrait, Chagall and Bella float above the ground, enraptured by each other's gaze. In her book of memoirs, *First Encounter*, Bella described how she was decorating Chagall's room with shawls and flowers for his birthday when he told her to stand still so that he could paint her: "You snatched the brushes, and squeezed out the paint, red, blue, white, transporting me in a stream of color. United we float over the decorated room, come to the window and want to fly out."

"She [Bella] has been haunting my paintings, the grand central image of my art."

Marc Chagall

Chagall the Commissar

▲ *Suprem atist Composition: White on White*, 1917-18, Kasimir Malevich.

KASIMIR MALEVICH

One of the most radical artists working in revolutionary Russia was Kasimir Malevich (1878-1935), a pioneer of abstract art. He experimented with a number of styles but wanted to "free art from the burden of the object" and developed a system of stark geometric abstraction called Suprematism.

Suprematism had a huge influence not just on painting but on commercial art, typography (lettering), furniture design, and architecture throughout Europe.

Malevich's most famous picture is *Suprematist Composition: White on White*, 1917-18 (above), a white square tilted on a square white canvas. In its powerful minimalism, it remains an important piece in 20th-century abstract art. Despite criticizing Chagall's figurative art, Malevich later adopted a more traditional style.

In 1917, Russian discontent with the war combined with hatred of the Czar led to the Russian Revolution (see page 22). Along with peasants and workers, Jews were given new civil rights. Chagall welcomed the freedom that the revolution seemed to promise. In *The Cemetery Gates* (right), he implies that Jews will reach "the promised land."

WORKING FOR THE REVOLUTION

Despite Bella's opposition, the usually apolitical Chagall showed his enthusiasm for the new regime by accepting a job in 1918 as Commissar for the Fine Arts in Vitebsk. He threw himself into his new role and organized a huge artistic celebration to mark the first anniversary of the Russian Revolution.

◄ The committee of the Vitebsk Academy of Fine Arts, 1919. Chagall sits third from left, his old teacher Yehuda Pen third from right.

In 1919, Chagall opened the Vitebsk Academy of Fine Arts. He employed a wide range of artists for the teaching staff, from traditionalists like his old teacher Yehuda Pen to the abstract artist Kasimir Malevich (see panel). Malevich bitterly opposed Chagall and his "old-fashioned" ideas. While Chagall was away, Malevich took over the school. Angry and hurt, Chagall left Vitebsk for good.

TIMELINE ▶

1917	1918	1919
February and October Revolutions in Russia. Chagall turns down a job as Head of Fine Arts in the new Ministry of Culture. Russia agrees to peace with Germany in November.	First monograph on Chagall is published by Abraham Efross and Jacob Tugendhold. Chagall appointed Commissar for the Fine Arts in Vitebsk. World War I ends.	Chagall opens Vitebsk Academy of Fine Arts. His work is exhibited in two rooms of "First State Revolutionary Art" at the Winter Palace in Petrograd.

The Cemetery Gates, 1917

oil on canvas, 34 ¹/₄ x 27 in (87 x 68.5 cm), Centre National d'Art et de Culture Georges Pompidou, Paris, Gift of Ida Chagall

Chagall has written in Hebrew above the gates of the Jewish cemetery the hopeful Old Testament words: "This saith the Lord God: Behold, O my people, I will open your graves and cause you to come up out of your graves and take you to the land of Israel." The splintering of the sky and trees into angular planes shows the influence of Cubism.

The Russian Revolution

The Russian Revolution did not happen suddenly. In 1905, protests and strikes had forced the Czar to form a Duma, or parliament. However, it had little power and the Czar's regime remained extremely repressive. Illegal opposition groups operated in secret. The largest of these was the Social Democratic Party, which followed the teachings of Karl Marx (1818-83). He believed there should be a socialist revolution in which the wealth of the country would be shared among the people.

RUSSIA AT WAR

Opposition to the Czar grew after Russia's disastrous role in World War I. Bad leadership and organization led to terrible losses with casualties running in the

▲ The Russian royal family with Czar Nicholas at its center. The Czar's failure to make meaningful reforms led to revolution and his eventual death and the death of his family in 1918. They were secretly killed by the Bolshevik Red Guards.

millions. The war put a great strain on the Russian economy, and riots began over food shortages. In March of 1917, Czar Nicholas sent troops to stop riots in Petrograd but the soldiers mutinied and joined the protesters. The Czar resigned and the Duma formed a Provisional Government. These events are referred to as the "February Revolution."

THE BOLSHEVIKS EMERGE

The new government was politically moderate and had

A NOTE ON DATES

At the time of the Russian Revolution, Russia still used the old-style calendar, which was 13 days behind the Western-style calendar we use today (the Gregorian calendar). This means that the Revolutions usually referred to as the "February" and "October" Revolutions took place in March and November 1917, respectively.

◄ Russian casualties in World War I were so bad that the army was forced to use child soldiers. Many children were taken prisoner by the Germans.

to face challenges from the Soviets or workers councils. The government could not solve Russia's economic crisis and became more and more unpopular. With the Czar gone there was political freedom which enabled a radical wing of the Social Democratic Party – the Bolsheviks – to gain popularity.

ALL POWER TO THE SOVIETS

The Bolshevik leader Vladimir Ilyich Lenin led the opposition to the Provisional Government, rallying support with the slogan "Peace! Bread! Land! All power to the Soviets!" On November 6, 1917, Bolshevik troops stormed the Winter Palace and seized power. Lenin quickly established a new government and began radical changes to Russian society – titles and rank were abolished; peasants were given the right to take land; and women were given equal rights.

COMMUNIST RULE

The future of the Russian people was far from bright. When the Bolshevik party failed to gain many votes in the elections in November, Lenin gave up the idea of parliamentary democracy. The communists (as the Bolsheviks now called themselves) would rule as a dictatorship. Their regime would eventually be as repressive as that of the Czars'.

The new communist government made peace with Germany, but gave up a lot of territory and resources in the peace treaty. Soon, discontent with communist rule led to a terrible civil war. The communists won in 1921, but Russia's economy was in ruins. The ordinary workers and peasants continued to suffer.

In 1922, the year in which Chagall left Russia for good, the country became the Union of Soviet Socialist Republics (U.S.S.R).

◀ This Communist poster, created after 1922, shows the hammer and sickle – symbols of the urban workers and rural peasants. They were combined to become the symbol of the U.S.S.R. Lenin, the first leader of the U.S.S.R, is also shown (top left).

Disapproval and Departure

▲ *The Drowned Woman*, 1928, Marc Chagall.
Chagall initially painted this illustration for one of
La Fontaine's Fables in gouache, a type of water-
color. Later this was used to make an etching.

ILLUSTRATIONS AND ETCHINGS

Back in France, Chagall took on several
commissions from the art dealer and
publisher Ambroise Vollard (1866-1939).
These commissions not only gave Chagall
some income, but enabled him to develop
his etching technique, which he had begun
to do in Berlin. One of the projects was
illustrating the *Fables* of La Fontaine
(1621-95). Chagall initially created the
images with gouache, or opaque colors.
These were later engraved onto copper
plates to be printed in a book of limited-
edition etchings; Chagall hand-finished all
8,500 prints in color.

In May of 1920, Chagall and his family moved to
Moscow, where he painted a series of huge murals
for the State Jewish Chamber Theatre. Dancers,
musicians, actors, acrobats, fiddlers, traditional
Jewish figures – and Chagall himself – were shown
cavorting against a geometric background. Chagall
considered it among his best work but the
communist authorities disapproved. They saw it as
self-indulgent and irrelevant to Russian society.
They refused to pay him and, despite his fame,
sidelined him into a lowly job teaching drawing to
war orphans. Chagall decided to leave the country.

▶ Chagall
teaching in an
orphan colony in
Russia. Despite
the job's lowly
status, Chagall
"delighted" in
the children's
drawings.

STOLEN WORKS OF ART

In 1923, after spending a year in Berlin, Chagall took
his family back to France, where he stayed for almost
20 years. In both Berlin and Paris he was devastated
to find that many of the early works, which had
brought him fame, had been stolen or lost. Initially,
he painted replicas to replace them. As he settled
down, he began to explore France and experiment
with new techniques. The sense of peace he enjoyed
is expressed in *The Acrobat* (right).

TIMELINE ▶

1920	1921	1922	1923	1926
Chagall leaves Vitebsk for Moscow. He paints murals for Moscow's Jewish Theatre.	Chagall teaches drawing to war orphans. He begins his autobiography.	Chagall and family leave Russia for Berlin. He makes 20 etchings for his autobiography.	Chagall returns to Paris. He paints numerous replicas and variants of early works that were lost in his absence.	Chagall's first solo show is organized in the U.S. at the Reinhardt Gallery in New York. He begins work on illustrations for La Fontaine's *Fables*.

The Acrobat, 1930

oil on canvas, 40 x 29 in (117 x 73.5 cm), Centre National d'Art et de Culture Georges Pompidou, Paris, France

In 1927, after the two friends had been to the Winter Circus in Paris together, Ambroise Vollard commissioned Chagall to do a series of 19 gouaches on a circus theme. The subject became a favorite for Chagall. His circus pictures are touched with a moving sense of magic, poetry, and personal drama. The dreaminess of this charming image is accentuated by a softer, blurred technique.

"I always regarded clowns, acrobats, and actors as tragic figures, which for me resemble the figures in religious paintings."

Marc Chagall

Visiting the Holy Land

▲ Chagall shortly after the publication of his autobiography, *My Life*. Bella and Chagall worked closely together on the French edition of the book, discussing the translation from Yiddish line by line.

THE ARTIST'S AUTOBIOGRAPHY

In 1931, the same year the Chagalls visited Palestine, Chagall's autobiography, *Ma Vie* (*My Life*) was published. It had taken ten years to come together. Chagall began writing it in Russia and took it to Berlin in 1922. Here, the art publisher Paul Cassirer (1871-1926) suggested that he publish it in German and illustrate it with etchings. Although Cassirer produced a printed edition of the 20 etchings of scenes from Chagall's youth, the book itself proved difficult to translate, which is why it was not published until 1931. It was translated from the original Yiddish (Jewish) by Bella Chagall and a young writer Jean Paulhan (1884-1968). An English version was published in 1965.

While working on his autobiography (see panel), the *Fables*, and other projects, Chagall had mastered the art of etching and made it his own. Vollard was so impressed that he gave Chagall an even more important commission – to illustrate the Bible.

A BIBLICAL LANDSCAPE

Chagall had always been fascinated by the Bible. Now he wanted to gain first-hand experience of the biblical homeland of the Jews. Invited by the mayor of Tel Aviv, Chagall and his family went to the Holy Land early in 1931. They traveled via Egypt and Lebanon to spend several months in Palestine (Israel did not exist as a country then).

Chagall was inspired by his visit. It sparked many works, such as *Solitude* (right), in addition to his Bible illustrations. However, the Bible project was interrupted by World War II and would not be ready for publication until 1956.

▲ The rocky landscape of the Holy Land is very dramatic. Chagall was inspired by seeing Biblical holy places first hand.

TIMELINE ▶

1930	1931	1932	1933	1934
Commissioned by Vollard, Chagall starts to illustrate the Bible.	Chagall spends three months in Palestine. His autobiography *Ma Vie* is published.	Chagall's first exhibition in the Netherlands. He travels to Amsterdam.	A number of Chagall's works are publicly burned by the Nazis.	Chagall travels around Spain.

Solitude, 1933-34

oil on canvas, 37 4/5 x 62 1/5 in (96 x 158 cm), Tel Aviv Museum of Art, Tel Aviv, Israel

In this dark and gloomy painting, familiar motifs in Chagall's art – the cow, the fiddle, and Russian houses – surround a huge figure of a traditional Jew lost in thought as he clutches a Torah scroll (the most sacred text of the Jews). A little white angel flies against a pale blue sky. The figure of the Jew is isolated, exiled like the Jews of Europe. Chagall donated the painting to the Tel Aviv Museum of Art.

*"Will God or someone else give me the strength
to breathe the breath of prayer and mourning
into my paintings, the breath of prayer
for redemption and resurrection?"*

Marc Chagall, My Life

Tensions in Europe

▲ Jews in Poland are rounded up by German soldiers in 1943.

NAZI ANTI-SEMITISM

Adolf Hitler (1889-1945) and the Nazi (National Socialist) party came to power in Germany in 1933, when the country was in a deep economic depression. Hitler blamed most of Germany's problems on the Jewish people, and his government was dedicated to the persecution of the Jews.

First Jews were banned from civil service and journalism, then excluded from the armed forces and higher education. By 1938, when Chagall painted *The White Crucifixion*, the Nazi policy became even more repressive and violent. Jews were confined to concentration camps and used as forced labor. Then in 1941, under the cover of World War II, the Nazis began killing Jews in a planned extermination which became known as the Holocaust. By 1945, six million Jews, three-quarters of all the Jews in Europe, had been murdered.

In 1935, Chagall traveled to Vilnius (then in Poland, now the capital of Lithuania), where he was guest of honor at the opening of the Jewish Cultural Institute.

HATRED OF THE JEWS

The visit to Poland made Chagall very aware of the rise of anti-Semitism, or anti-Jewish feelings, in Europe, especially in Nazi Germany (see panel). By the mid-1930s, Nazi anti-Semitism affected Chagall personally. All of his works were removed from German museums and in 1937 – the year in which Chagall became a French citizen – three of them were shown in the Nazis' Degenerate Art exhibition.

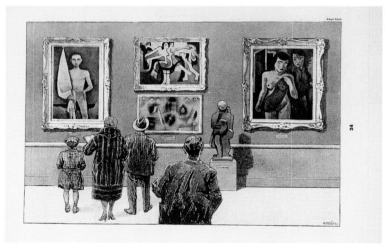

▲ This illustration shows the Nazis' Degenerate Art exhibition held in 1937. Its aim was to ridicule art that did not conform with Nazi beliefs.

A CRY OF PROTEST

The White Crucifixion was painted in 1938. It was Chagall's reaction to the Nazi persecution of the Jewish people. Some Jews were offended by his use of Christian imagery but Chagall saw Jesus, who was also a Jew, as a symbol of all suffering Jews.

TIMELINE ▶

1935	1937	1938
Chagall travels to Vilnius, then in Poland (now in Lithuania). He visits Warsaw and sees the threat to the Jewish population.	Chagall travels to Italy. All his works are removed from German museums by the Nazis and three are shown at the Degenerate Art Exhibition. Chagall becomes a French citizen.	Chagall exhibits in Brussels. He paints *The White Crucifixion*.

The White Crucifixion, 1938

oil on canvas, 60 3/4 x 55 in (154.3 x 139.7 cm), The Art Institute of Chicago, Chicago, Illinois

Around the central figure of the crucified Christ, Chagall has painted a variety of scenes that show Jewish suffering. A village is attacked and burned by Nazi soldiers; all around are frightened, fleeing, or lamenting Jewish figures. A wandering Jew clutching a Torah symbolizes the homeless Jews as in *Solitude* (see page 27). There is also a burning Torah (bottom right). In the early 1930s, Chagall had traveled around Europe and seen many paintings by the Old Masters, for whom the crucifixion was a standard subject. By borrowing a central image from traditional Christian art, Chagall might be indicating that the persecution of the Jews is a universal outrage that affects everyone, regardless of their religion or race.

Exile in America

ARTISTS IN EXILE

Many artists, writers, composers, and intellectuals fled Europe, especially occupied France, during World War II. Many found a safe haven in New York, as Chagall did.

These European artists were warmly welcomed and a number of exhibitions were held in their honor. At his New York gallery, Pierre Matisse (1899-1989, son of the artist Henri Matisse), organized the "Artists in Exile" exhibition. He gave Chagall, among others, several one-man shows. In addition, the Museum of Modern Art put on an "Art in Exile" exhibition, while the Whitney Museum held an exhibition called "European Artists in America."

▲ This 1940s postcard conveys the excitement of New York through its famous skyline, with the Empire State Building in the center.

When World War II began in 1939, the Chagalls were living outside Paris. In 1940 they moved to southern France, arriving in the village of Gordes at the same time as the German army occupied Paris. They lived there for about a year, but like all Jews in France, they were in danger of being caught and taken to a concentration camp. In 1941, the Museum of Modern Art in New York sent Chagall an invitation to come to the United States.

LEAVING FRANCE

On June 23, 1941, the Chagalls sailed into New York. They brought with them Chagall's work packed up in crates and trunks. He was determined never to suffer the loss of his work as he had in 1914 (see page 24).

Despite not speaking English, Chagall was soon happily settled in New York. A one-man show of his work received rave reviews (see panel) and commissions for theater and ballet designs followed. During this period, Chagall painted a number of canvases showing horrific scenes of war, but also painted more optimistic images such as *The Juggler* (right).

▲ Chagall's first exhibition at the Pierre Matisse Gallery, New York, 1941.

TIMELINE ▶

1939	1940	1941	1942
Shortly before the outbreak of World War II in September, Chagall and his family leave Paris for the Loire Valley.	The Chagalls move further south to Gordes in the Vaucluse mountains. Chagall receives an invitation to go to the U.S. from the Museum of Modern Art in New York.	The Chagalls leave France. Chagall has his first U.S. exhibition at Pierre Matisse's gallery in New York.	Chagall spends the summer in Mexico, working on ballet designs.

The Juggler, 1943

oil on canvas, 43 $\frac{1}{4}$ x 31 $\frac{1}{7}$ (109.9 x 79.1 cm), The Art Institute of Chicago, Chicago, Illinois

Part man, part bird, part angel, the flamboyant central figure dances in a circus ring with a clock (a traditional symbol of time passing and the inevitability of death) draped over one arm. Old Russian houses and a Jewish fiddler are among the secondary scenes. As usual with Chagall, it is impossible to read the symbolism precisely, but the painting seems to express the energy and variety of the human spirit.

New York Immigrants

When Marc Chagall sailed into New York harbor, he became one of the millions of immigrants who had fled poverty or persecution to find a new life in the U.S. For the Chagalls, and for millions of others, the first sight that greeted them was the Statue of Liberty. The base of the statue is inscribed with these idealistic, welcoming words, "Give me your tired, your poor…Your huddled masses, yearning to breathe free."

FIRST STOP – ELLIS ISLAND

Near Liberty Island, where the statue stands, is Ellis Island. Until 1954, this was where immigrants to the U.S. made their first stop, at the immigration center. They were interviewed and given medical checks before being admitted into the country. Some had to endure weeks or even months of waiting. In its 62-year history, 12 million immigrants passed through Ellis Island.

In the 19th and early 20th centuries,

▲ Immigrants to the U.S. on board a ship, c. 1915, cheer and throw their hats up as they see the Statue of Liberty.

huge numbers of immigrants arrived in the U.S. They came from South and Central America, Europe, Russia, and eastern Asia. On Ellis Island, once they had been permitted entry, they could buy cheap train tickets which allowed them to travel on to cities such as Chicago and San Francisco.

▼ Immigrants line up at Ellis Island, c. 1905, waiting to be admitted into the U.S. and to start a new life.

By 1898, when this picture was taken, the Jewish community was well established in the Lower East Side of New York. In this crowded Orchard Street market, some of the signs hanging from storefronts are written in Hebrew.

STICKING TOGETHER

Many immigrants chose to stay in New York, and the city became a rich mix of cultures. Particular groups tended to move into the same areas, as the names Chinatown and Little Italy imply.

Around the time of Chagall's birth, the first boatloads of Eastern European immigrants were settling in the crowded streets of the Lower East Side of Manhattan. Between 1870 and 1920, when new immigration laws reduced the number of immigrants, millions of Russians, Slavs, Poles, and Lithuanians settled here. Often two or three families would share an apartment in the five-story tenement blocks. This became the Jewish center of the city. Yiddish was the language spoken here most, and there were about 500 synagogues.

"I am impressed by the greatness of this country [America] and the feeling of freedom that it gives me."

Marc Chagall

HOME FROM HOME

Chagall, who never learned English but always spoke Yiddish, Russian, or French, felt at home on the Lower East Side. He loved the Jewish food and the Yiddish newspapers he could buy. By now he was wealthy and could afford to live in a more expensive area. At first he and Bella stayed in hotels, but to have the peace and space to paint they moved to an apartment on 74th Street on Manhattan's Upper West Side.

The Death of Bella

▲ Ida Chagall in 1945. She is standing beside one of her father's paintings of her mother, *My Fiancée in Black Gloves*, 1909.

IDA CHAGALL (1916-94)

Bella and Marc Chagall's only child, Ida, had a very close relationship with her father. In her adult years she was dedicated to supporting him and promoting his international reputation. She handled his business affairs, organized exhibitions, and spoke with journalists and publishers. She even sewed the costumes for his stage designs – as her mother had done before her.

In 1934, at age 18, she married a young lawyer named Michel Gorday, but the couple later divorced. In 1952, she married the art historian Franz Meyer who wrote an important study about Chagall.

Ida was responsible for introducing her father to the two women in his life following Bella's death – Virginia Haggard and Valentina (Vava) Brodsky (see page 36).

The Chagalls sometimes left the city to stay in the country at Cranberry Lake in upstate New York. While here they heard that Paris had been liberated from the Nazis on August 25, 1944. Bella felt lonely in New York and was looking forward to returning to Paris. However, it was not meant to be. On September 2, 1944, she died suddenly of an infection.

Chagall was devastated. "Everything has grown dark before my eyes," he wrote. Their daughter, Ida, brought him to live with her at her New York apartment. He turned his canvases to the wall, and for nine months painted nothing.

FINDING NEW PURPOSE

Eventually Chagall moved back into his own home and began to work again. He was painting *Around Her* (right) when he met Virginia Haggard McNeil, whom Ida had arranged to be his housekeeper. The two gradually fell in love and were together for seven years. They had a son, David, but their relationship was not known about publicly until after Chagall's death.

◄ This photograph of Chagall with Virginia and their son in 1951 appeared in *My Life with Chagall, Seven Years of Plenty*. This revealing book was written by Virginia and published in 1986, the year after Chagall's death.

TIMELINE ▶

1944	1945	1946	1947
Paris is liberated from the Germans. Bella dies suddenly.	World War II ends. Virginia Haggard becomes Chagall's housekeeper. Chagall designs sets and costumes for Stravinsky's ballet *The Firebird*, staged in New York.	Museum of Modern Art in New York holds a Chagall retrospective. On June 22, Virginia gives birth to Chagall's son David.	Musée National d'Art Moderne in Paris holds a retrospective. Chagall travels to Paris. Exhibits work in Amsterdam, London, and Zürich.

Around Her, 1945

oil on canvas, 51 1/2 x 43 1/6 in (131 x 109.7 cm), Centre National d'Art et de Culture Georges Pompidou, Paris, France

Here Chagall's blues, usually so rich and vibrant, are dark and muted, reflecting the bereaved artist's sadness. Bella weeps quietly (right) while Chagall paints. His head – like his world – is turned upside down. The images form a circular movement, an acrobat swoops down, the bridal couple fly up, and a crystal ball at the center reveals memories of Vitebsk.

Vava and Vence

A PAINTER AT THE OPÉRA

In 1963, the French government invited Chagall to paint the ceiling of the Paris Opéra. Some critics objected to the idea of a Russian Jew decorating this French national monument, while others thought that modern art was wrong for a 19th-century building. Nearly everyone agreed that the result was a masterpiece.

It was a huge undertaking. Chagall painted over 2,368 square feet (220 sq m) of canvas, which were glued to panels of polyester and then hoisted to the ceiling. Once the panels were in position, the 77-year-old artist climbed 75 feet (23 m) of scaffolding to reach the ceiling and touch up details. When the ceiling painting was first seen on September 23, 1964, one critic wrote, "For once, the best seats in the house were in the uppermost circle."

After seven years in the United States, Chagall was ready to return to France. In 1948, he and Virginia moved into a house outside Paris. They also traveled to Italy and the Côte d'Azur in southern France, where Picasso and Matisse were living. Chagall loved the Côte d'Azur, and in 1950, he bought "La Colline," a beautiful house with a huge studio overlooking the Mediterranean Sea at Vence.

In 1951, Chagall and Virginia separated. The following year Ida introduced her father to Valentina Brodsky (Vava). In July of 1952, they married.

▶ Chagall with Vava in 1962. They remained together happily until Chagall's death. At Vava's request, Chagall's relationship with Virginia was never made public.

MONUMENTAL WORK

From the 1950s onward, Chagall often worked on a monumental scale, including projects like the Paris Opéra (see panel). He discovered a run-down chapel in Vence, and spent some 20 years on a series of large paintings called the "Biblical Messsage" for it. When it proved impossible to install the paintings in the chapel, Chagall donated them to the city of Nice where a museum was opened in 1973 to house them.

▲ The ceiling of the Paris Opéra, 1964.

TIMELINE ▶

1948	1950	1951	1952	1955	1956	1957	1964
Chagall returns to live in France, initially outside Paris.	Chagall moves to Vence. He meets lithographer Charles Sorlier.	Chagall exhibits in Israel. He separates from Virginia Haggard.	Chagall meets Valentina Brodsky (Vava), whom he marries on July 12.	Chagall begins "Biblical Message" paintings.	Chagall's Bible etchings finally published.	Designs wall mosaics and stained-glass windows.	Chagall paints the ceiling of the Paris Opéra.

Abraham and the Three Angels, 1960-66

oil on canvas, 74 4/5 x 115 in (190 x 292 cm), Musée National Message Biblique, Nice, France

Almost 10 feet (3 m) long, this magnificent canvas is one of the paintings in the Biblical Message series. There were seventeen pictures in the series, featuring episodes from three different biblical books: Genesis, Exodus, and the Song of Solomon. This scene shows the episode in Genesis where Abraham gives hospitality – rest, food, and drink – to three angels of God. In return, they promise him that his wife, Sarah, will conceive a child despite her age. Painted when Chagall was in his seventies, it shows the striking vibrancy of color and poetic power that characterize his work throughout his life.

"Ever since early childhood, I have been captivated by the Bible. It has always seemed to me, and still seems today, the greatest source of poetry imaginable."

Marc Chagall

A Productive Old Age

◀ **The Artist in His Studio, 1976.** Chagall produced about 1,100 lithographs such as this one during his career.

Chagall's late years were remarkably productive – as well as painting, he made lithographs, stained-glass windows, monumental mosaics, ceramics, sculptures, and tapestries. He was applauded as one of the greatest living artists of the 20th century.

LITHOGRAPHY

Lithography is a printing technique where the image is originally drawn or painted on stone. Chagall produced more than a thousand lithographs. For many years, from 1950 until his death, he worked closely with expert lithographer Charles Sorlier. Sorlier prepared the lithographic stones for Chagall, eventually replacing the traditional limestone plates with copper ones.

Before he met Sorlier (who became like a son to him), Chagall had made only black-and-white lithographs, but Sorlier had the technical expertise to allow him to bring his glorious sense of color to the medium. Indeed, the brilliant color Chagall achieved in lithography seems to have had an effect on his use of color in paintings and stained glass.

RETURNING TO RUSSIA

In 1973, Chagall, age 86, was invited by the Soviet Culture Minister to visit Russia. It was the first time he had returned there since 1922. The authorities organized an exhibition in Moscow to celebrate the event, at which Chagall was asked to sign the murals for the Jewish Theatre rejected 50 years before (see page 24). The old Russian artist was moved to tears.

Major exhibitions of Chagall's work continued to be held through the 1980s, including one at London's Royal Academy. The 97-year-old Chagall was too frail to attend its opening in January 1985. Two months later, on the evening of March 28, after spending all day at work on a lithograph, he died peacefully of old age.

◀ Chagall signs autographs for the admirers that surround him in Moscow, 1973.

TIMELINE ▶

1966	1969	1973	1977	March 28, 1985
Chagall and Vava move to Saint-Paul-de-Vence.	Foundation stone for Biblical Message museum laid. "Hommáge a Marc Chagall" exhibition of 474 works at Grand Palais in Paris.	Chagall visits Russia for the first time in 50 years. Reunited with two of his sisters.	Chagall is awarded France's highest honor, the Grand Cross of the Legion of Honour. Chagall exhibition at the Louvre: the first ever for a living artist.	Chagall dies at his home in Saint-Paul-de-Vence.

"There is something very simple about a stained-glass window: just materials and light."

Marc Chagall

The Arts to the Glory of God, 1978

stained-glass window,125 x 54 1/2 in (317.5 x 138.4 cm), Chichester Cathedral, West Sussex, England

Chagall did not even begin to make stained-glass windows until he was almost 70, yet he is acknowledged – along with Matisse – as one of the 20th-century masters of this art form. This window for Chichester Cathedral was completed when Chagall was over 90 years old. It takes its inspiration from Psalm 150 and is usually described by the Psalm's last line, "Let everything that hath breath, praise the Lord." Stained glass is an appropriate medium for Chagall. The effect of light shining through colored glass is close to the luminous quality he strived to achieve in his painting.

Chagall's Legacy

Marc Chagall was buried in the Catholic cemetery in Saint-Paul-de-Vence, the village where he died. Some protested that he should have been buried in a Jewish cemetery, but this contradiction is just one of many that makes up the artist Chagall. He was a Russian and a Frenchman; a Jew who held many beliefs that were not Jewish.

These contradictions can be found in his work – in the cultural mix of his imagery; in the sense of joy that is often tinged with sadness; in the harmonious order he creates from his jumble of subjects. It is this perhaps that makes his art so universally popular. In his struggle to create a new reality which embraces all these contradictions, Chagall reflects the struggle we all face, but gives us hope in the sense of celebration and unity he achieves.

"In the arts, as in life, everything is possible provided it is based on love."

Marc Chagall

▲ *Son of Man*, 1964, René Magritte. One of the Surrealists, Magritte (1898-1967) uses images such as the derby hat again and again, like the repeated images in Chagall's work.

WORKING APART

Chagall remained outside the major art movements of the 20th century. He flirted with Cubism and Orphism but always kept his own unique style. In the 1920s, Chagall was asked to join the Surrealists, but he refused. This group of artists and writers expressed the world of dreams and the unconscious mind. To do this the Surrealists often used everyday objects as symbols, or metaphors, of ideas, something Chagall had done before them. Surrealism's founder André Breton (1896-1966) recognized Chagall's influence, writing that, through him, "metaphor made its triumphant entry into modern painting."

▲ Chagall's mosaic *The Prophet Elijah* at the Biblical Message Museum in Nice. Chagall felt the work in the museum was relevant to everyone regardless of their religious beliefs.

► *Life*, c. 1990, Yvette Cauquil-Prince. This magnificent tapestry was produced some five years after Chagall's death. In it many of his favorite themes can be seen – circus performers, loving couples, musicians – pictured on a dramatic scale. The huge tapestry measures 142 x 191 in (361 x 485 cm).

ART AND CRAFT

In his later years, Chagall embarked on many projects – stained-glass, lithography, and tapestry – which required the technical skills of crafts people. One such person was master-craftswoman Yvette Cauquil-Prince (b. 1928), a tapestry maker whom Chagall met in 1964. She had been producing tapestries based on works of art by many 20th-century masters. Chagall collaborated with her and she continued to produce tapestries from his designs even after his death. Although the images already existed in other forms, the different technique and the change in scale meant that an entirely new work of art was created, giving new life to Chagall's work.

STILL IN THE SPOTLIGHT

Chagall's work continues to find new admirers today. Greeting cards and posters of his popular works sell in the thousands. The original art can be seen in museums and galleries around the world – as well as in many other public places such as cathedrals and synagogues, government buildings, theaters, and universities. People continue to enjoy Chagall's own unique vision of life in all its variety.

"A poet with the wings of a painter."
Novelist Henry Miller talking about Chagall

◄ Chagall with Yvette Cauquil-Prince, c. 1966.

Poems Between Friends

Chagall has been described as a "poet with the wings of a painter," because his whole approach to art has a poetic quality. This may be one of the reasons why many of his friends were poets. Chagall himself wrote poetry. His prose and even his way of talking were poetic – colorful and full of images.

▼ *My Land*, 1946, by Marc Chagall. These are extracts from a poem Chagall wrote soon after the end of World War II.

Only that land is mine
That lies in my soul.
As a native, with no documents
I enter that land...

Gardens are blooming inside me,
My flowers I invented,
My own streets -
But there are no houses.
They have been destroyed since my childhood.
Their inhabitants stray in the air,
Seek a dwelling,
They live in my soul...

DEDICATED TO CHAGALL

A number of Chagall's poet friends wrote poems to and about him, both in his early years as a struggling young artist in Paris, and later. When he was living at La Ruche (see pages 12-15), he became close to the poet Blaise Cendrars, who dedicated several poems to Chagall, including *Portrait* (below).

He's asleep
He wakes up
Suddenly, he paints
He takes a church and paints
*   with a church*
He takes a cow and paints
*   with a cow*
With a sardine
With heads, hands, knives...

Chagall is astonished to still
*   be alive.*

▲ Extract from *Portrait*, 1913, by Blaise Cendrars.

TIMELINE ▶

1887	1909	1914	1916	1919
July 7 Moyshe Segal (Marc Chagall) born in Vitebsk.	**1909** Enrolls at Zvantseva School. He meets Bella Rosenfeld, his future wife.	**May** Travels to Berlin for his first one-man exhibition at Der Sturm gallery.	**May 18** Ida Chagall born.	**1919** Opens Vitebsk Academy of Fine Arts.
1906 Enters Yehuda Pen's art school in Vitebsk.	**1910** Moves to Paris. Sees modern French art for first time.	**June** Exhibition opens to good reviews. Chagall travels on to Russia.	**November** Exhibits in Moscow with the avant-garde association of artists, "Knave of Diamonds."	**1920** Leaves Vitebsk for Moscow. Paints murals for Moscow's Jewish Theatre.
Winter 1906-07 Moves to St. Petersburg.	**1911** Moves into the artists' colony La Ruche (the Beehive). Meets the poets Blaise Cendrars and Guillaume Apollinaire.	**August** World War I has begun. Chagall stranded in Vitebsk.	**1917** Russian Revolution. Chagall turns down job offer as Head of Fine Arts in the new Ministry of Culture.	**1921** Teaches drawing to war orphans. Begins his autobiography.
1907 Enrolls in School of the Imperial Society for the Protection of the Fine Arts.		**1915** Marries Bella in Vitebsk on July 25. Works at the War Economy Office in Petrograd.	**1918** Appointed Commissar for the Fine Arts in Vitebsk. World War I ends.	**1922** Chagalls leave Russia for Berlin. He makes etchings for autobiography.
1908 Leaves the Imperial Society school. Meets Maxim Vinaver.	**1912-13** Has paintings exhibited in Paris.			**1923** Returns to Paris.

*Your scarlet face your biplane convertible
    into hydroplane
Your round house where a smoked
    herring swims...*

*And I began to cry reminiscing over our
    childhoods
And you show me a dreadful purple
This little painting where there is a cart
    which reminded me of the day
A day made out of pieces of mauves yellows
    blues greens and reds...
Two gold rings near some sandals
Kindle the sun
While your hair is like the trolley cable
Across Europe arrayed in little many-colored
    fires.*

◀ **Extract from *Rotsoge*, for the painter Marc Chagall, 1914 by Guillaume Apollinaire.**

▼ ***To Marc Chagall**, 1950, by Paul Éluard.*

*Donkey or cow cock or horse
Even the shell of a violin
A singing man a single bird
Agile dancing man with woman*

*A couple drenched in its
    own spring*

*Gold of grass lead of sky
Separated by blue flames
A little health a little dew
Rainbowed blood and
    tolling heart*

A couple the first gleam of day

*Catacombed beneath the snow
A vine in opulence outlines
A countenance with lips of moon
That has not ever slept at night.*

POETRY INSPIRED BY PAINTING

While living at La Ruche, Chagall also met the poet and critic Guillaume Apollinaire, who was a leading figure in the avant-garde and a passionate supporter of Cubism. Chagall was worried that Apollinaire would not like his work, but when the poet visited the artist's studio, he apparently murmured "Supernatural." He wrote to Chagall the next day, enclosing the poem above. Later, another poet, Paul Éluard (1895-1952), a leading figure in the Surrealists, was also inspired by Chagall's art (right).

1926	1937	1946	1952	1969
1926 First U.S. solo show. Begins work on illustrations for La Fontaine's *Fables*.	**1937** Works shown at the Degenerate Art Exhibition. Becomes a French citizen.	**1946** Museum of Modern Art in New York hold retrospective. On June 22, son David born.	**1952** Meets and marries Valentina Brodsky (Vava).	**1969** Work begins on Biblical Message museum.
1930 Begins work on illustrating the Bible.	**1939** World War II begins.	**1947** Retrospectives held in Paris, Amsterdam, London, Zürich, and Berne.	**1955** Begins "Biblical Message" paintings.	**1973** Chagall visits Russia for first time in 50 years.
1931 Spends three months in Palestine.	**1941** Leaves France for U.S. Exhibition at Pierre Matisse's gallery, New York.	**1948** Returns to live in France.	**1956** Bible etchings finally published.	**1977** Awarded France's highest honor, the Grand Cross of the Legion of Honour. Given exhibition at Louvre – the first ever of a living artist.
1933 His autobiography, *Ma Vie*, is published.	**1944** Bella dies suddenly.	**1950** Moves to Vence.	**1957** Designs his first stained-glass window.	
1934 Travels in Spain.	**1945** World War II ends. Meets Virginia Haggard. Designs for Stravinsky's ballet *The Firebird*.	**1951** Travels to Israel. Separates from Virginia.	**1964** Paints the ceiling of the Paris Opéra.	**March 28, 1985** Chagall dies at his home in Saint-Paul-de-Vence.
1935 Travels to Poland. Sees threat to European Jews.			**1966** Moves short distance to Saint-Paul-de-Vence.	

Glossary

abstract art: a style of painting or drawing pictures that are independent of reality; such pictures may sometimes be based on a landscape, person, or some other object seen in the real world, but are made up of colors and lines used for their own sake.

avant-garde: describes new, experimental, or radical ideas. From the French for vanguard, the first troops into battle.

The Blue Riders: a group of Expressionists formed in 1911. The members, who included Wassily Kandinsky (1866-1944), Paul Klee (1879-1940), Franz Marc (1880-1916), and August Macke (1887-1914), had different artistic styles. They were united in their attempts to use color in a new way and to capture a spiritual value in their work.

Bolshevik: a member of the Russian Communist Party.

Cubism: the name of an art movement based in Paris from about 1907, led by Pablo Picasso and Georges Braque. The Cubists painted multiple viewpoints of people or objects so the viewpoints could all be seen at once.

degenerate: something that has descended to a low moral, mental, or artistic level.

empire: a large number of countries ruled by a more powerful country.

etching: a print on paper made from an engraved metal plate.

Expressionism: an approach to painting which communicates an emotional state of mind rather than external reality.

Fauves: French for "wild beasts," the name given by a shocked critic in 1905 to a group of painters, including Henri Matisse (1869-1954) and Andre Derain (1880-1954), who used bright, unnatural colors in their art.

gouache: opaque, or non-transparent, watercolors that have been mixed with water and gum.

lithograph: a print on paper made from a special stone on which an image has been drawn or painted.

minimalist: using extremely simple, abstract forms.

Orphism: an art movement that developed out of Cubism in the early 20th century, led by the French painter Robert Delaunay (1885-1941). It was characterized by a more vibrant use of color.

palette: a flat board on which artists arrange their oil paints for use. Also, the range of colors used in painting.

patron: someone who supports an artist financially by buying their work or giving them money.

portrait: an image of a person's face, which sometimes tries to capture something of their personality.

retrospective: an exhibition showing the development of an artist's work over his or her lifetime.

Rococo: a style of art that emerged in France in the early 18th century. It was characterized by light brushstrokes and playful imagery. Francois Boucher was one of the greatest Rococo artists.

ruble: the Russian unit of money.

Salon: annual art exhibition organized by the French Academy. In the 19th century the jury refused works by many Impressionist and Post-Impressionist painters who then exhibited at the Salon des Refusés. The Salon des Indépendants was started in 1884.

Suprematism: a highly influential Russian art movement started by Kasimir Malevich in 1915. Paintings were abstract, made up of pure geometric shapes – the square, circle, rectangle, and triangle.

Surrealism: an intellectual movement that began in the 1920s, which tried to show the life of our unconscious minds and dreams. Its most famous artist is Salvador Dali (1904-89), but it also included writers and film-makers.

symbols: something, such as an image of an object, that represents something else, such as an idea or an emotion.

Museums and Galleries

Works by Chagall are exhibited in museums, galleries and in some special buildings all around the world. Even if you can't visit any of these galleries yourself, you may be able to visit their web sites. Gallery web sites often show pictures of the artworks they have on display. Some of the web sites even offer virtual tours which allow you to wander around and look at different paintings while sitting comfortably in front of your computer!

Most of the international web sites detailed below include an option that allows you to view them in English.

EUROPE

Centre National d'Art et de Culture Georges Pompidou
75191 Paris
cedex 04
France
www.centrepompidou.fr

Chichester Cathedral
The Royal Chantry
Cathedral Cloisters
Chichester, West Sussex
PO19 1PX
England
www.fransnet.clara.net/chicath

Kunstmuseum, Berne
Sammlung Im Obersteg
Wichterheer-Gut Staatsstrasse
CH-3653
Switzerland
www.kunstmuseumbern.ch

Musée National Message Biblique Marc Chagall
Avenue Docteur
Ménard 06000
Nice, France
www.ac-nice.fr

Stedelijk Museum
Paulus Potterstraat 13
1071 CX Amsterdam
Post Box 75082
1070 AB Amsterdam
The Netherlands
www.stedelijk.nl

UNITED STATES

Art Institute of Chicago
111 South Michigan Avenue
Chicago, IL 60603-6110
www.artic.edu

Museum of Modern Art
(Under renovation until 2005. See web site for further details.)
11 West 53rd Street
New York, NY 10019
www.moma.org

Philadelphia Museum of Art
Benjamin Franklin Parkway and 26th Street
Philadelphia, PA 19130
www.philamuseum.org

San Diego Museum of Art
PO Box 122107
San Diego, CA 92112-2107
www.sandiegomuseum.org

Solomon R. Guggenheim Museum
1071 5th Avenue (at 89th Street)
New York, NY
www.guggenheimcollection.org

REST OF THE WORLD

The Israel Museum
POB 71117
Jerusalem 91710
Israel
www.imj.org.il

The State Russian Museum
Mikhailovsky Palace
Inzhenernaya Ulitsa 4
St. Petersburg
Russia
www.rusmuseum.ru/eng

Tel Aviv Museum of Art
27 Shaul Hamelech Boulevard
Tel Aviv 64329
Israel
www.tamuseum.com

Index